Growing as a Co-Laborer
WITH GOD IN WORLD MISSIONS

FAITH PROMISE
PRINCIPLES THAT
INCREASE FAITH

...Without faith it is impossible to please God...

DR. JAMES WILKINS

Foreword
By Dr. Clifford Clark
A man God has used to raise millions for the cause of missions

Dr. James Wilkins, one of the major thinkers and writers for biblical based, Baptist churches, has written this introductory book (for all age groups) on Missionary Faith Promise giving. **Dr Wilkins correlates "tithing" and "faith promise" mission giving** for our spiritual life now and at the "Judgment Seat of Christ" where Christians will receive their rewards from Jesus Christ.

Dr. Wilkins sees **the "big picture" and the foundational biblical principles of giving by faith.** Not only will these principles increase your faith but also enlarge the numbers of missionary on the field.

Every Person "young or old" should read and study this book prior to a mission emphasis in the local church. This book should also be studied by all missionary candidates in mission courses, and the leaders in the local church under direction of the pastor.

Yours for Souls Everywhere

Clifford E. Clark, Servant of World Missions

Copyright © 2009 Dr. James Wilkins. All rights reserved.

Writings contained herein are by the author unless otherwise stated.

No part of this publication may be reproduced, stored in a retrieval system or transmitted in any way by any means—electronic, mechanical, photocopy, recording or otherwise—without the prior permission of the copyright holder, except as provided by USA copyright law.

Printed in the United States of America.

All Scriptures are taken from the King James Bible.

ISBN # 978-1-935075-42-4

Printed by Calvary Publishing
A Ministry of Parker Memorial Baptist Church
1902 East Cavanaugh Road, Lansing, Michigan 48910
www.CalvaryPublishing.org

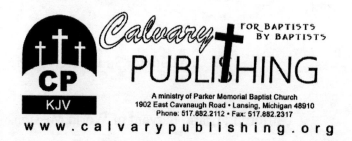

A ministry of Parker Memorial Baptist Church
1902 East Cavanaugh Road • Lansing, Michigan 48910
Phone: 517.882.2112 • Fax: 517.882.2317
www.calvarypublishing.org

TABLE OF CONTENTS

LESSON ONE
HOW TO HAVE SOMETHING IN HEAVEN WHEN YOU GET THERE.

These lessons show how one can convert his earthly treasures and obey God's command of …"lay up for yourself treasures in heaven."

Page 13

LESSON TWO
MY FIRST FAITH PROMISE MISSIONS CONFERENCE

One must do each daily exercise in this story in order to get the principle through his mind and on into his soul so the principle will direct his life.

Page 35

LESSON THREE
HOW WOULD YOU LIKE TO HAVE JOY AND MULTIPLY YOUR INVESTMENTS?

As the giver obeys God, he becomes a channel of blessing to lost people to receive Christ as their Saviour. God's marvelous grace then makes these people a channel of blessing back to the giver.

Page 53

LESSON FOUR
YOUR FINANCIAL OBLIGATION TO GIVE UNDER THE GREAT COMMISSION

God has a chain of action in which he has revealed each Christian's part in world missions. This lesson deals with the tremendous obligation and reward promised to each individual member.

Page 83

SIMPLE STEPS TO USING THIS BOOK

Read this introduction to the book. This will give you some background information as to why this book was written. Next read over the "Dear Sunday School" letter and fill in the blanks on the Prayer List Page.

Go over the "Daily Declaration" and "Memory Verse" each morning and evening.

This book is designed with a grading procedure. You, as the Sunday School Class member, are to read each daily assignment on the day assigned before answering any of the questions. Then fill in the blanks on the day designated: Monday's on Monday, Tuesday's on Tuesday, etc. The answer to each question is found in the text by the symbol **(+)**.

This grading system in on the honor system.

    A = Excellent: Did the work on a daily basis.
    B = Good: Did all the work, but not on a daily basis.
    J = Future Judgment: Did not complete all the blanks.

The same procedure is followed each week.

A LETTER TO EACH STUDENT

Dear Sunday School Member,

In a very short time your church will begin its annual *Faith Promise Conference*. There will be heart touching slides of people in far off lands. You will be able to see the despair in some of their faces. If you look closely you can detect the hopelessness in others.

It is through Faith Promise Conferences, much like the one your church will be conducting, that average Sunday School members **are transformed into vibrant growing Christians** who are laying up their treasures in the bank of heaven.

LOOK AROUND YOU ...

Other members have learned to trust and obey God's word by faith. You can tell that they possess something that most people do not have... **peace, as well as confidence** and a more settled response when troubles or sorrows **invade their lives**.

In this **Faith Promise Conference you too can learn to become a co-laborer with God** and begin the process that leads to God's greatest blessings for you and your family.

The simple steps to experiencing some of God's choice blessings are:

First, complete your Sunday School lesson **every single day of the week**. Do the exercises on the day assigned **and review them every day.** State the daily declaration and attempt to memorize the memory verse.

Second, work every one of the four lessons and **strive to make an "A" each week.**

Third, when the Faith Promise Conference begins, attend **every service** possible.

Fourth, attempt to meet the missionaries and their families. **Have them over** to your home, if possible.

Fifth, pray about what God wants to give to you so you will be able to **invest it back** into Missions and getting the Gospel to a lost world.

Sixth, remember you are God's child and **he has promised** to help and bless you.

ONE OF THE MOST CHRIST-LIKE CHARACTERISTICS IS GIVING

Begin the process of developing that characteristic. I promise that you will become a much happier person if you will **take God as your financial partner** and follow his leading and advice.

IT IS NOT GIVING, BUT SOWING

"But this I say, He which soweth sparingly shall reap also sparingly; and he which soweth bountifully shall reap also bountifully." (II Cor 9:6)

We are not giving, but sowing when we invest money into the work of the Lord. You have invested in immortal, never dying souls, and your money **will keep working in their lives** until the Judgment Seat of Christ.

God challenges you to invest a lot in the lives of people. When you obey and sow as he directs you to by faith, then **he can supply you with the means to do so.** When you look to him by faith or loving trust as a child looks to her father, then HE IS SO HONORED AND OBLIGATED BY HIS PROMISE THAT HE DOES GREAT AND MIGHTY THINGS.

How to Begin your Prayer:
"OUR FATHER IN HEAVEN"

With the knowledge that the Bible commands each disciple to pray regularly and with a desire to pray more consistently in order to secure definite results, make the following prayer list.

Pray for These Things:

1. **I'll pray for myself**— for a humble, submissive spirit toward Christ.
2. **For my family** — that I may be a Christian testimony and a blessing to each one of them.
3. **For my pastor** — that God will give him the grace, spiritual power and wisdom to lead, feed, and shepherd the flock.
4. **For my country** —that God will send revival to our nation, especially to those in high positions.
5. **For our missionaries** — for their safety, success, and support. (Write down the missionaries' names and their countries.)
    1. _____ country _____
    2. _____ country _____
    3. _____ country _____

6. **For my lost loved ones and friends**. Write down at least three people whom you will pray for daily.
    1. _____ Date prayer answered _____
    2. _____ Date prayer answered _____
    3. _____ Date prayer answered _____

7. **For evangelists and other special workers**, call them by name. (Ex. James Wilkins)

How to Conclude: "IN JESUS' NAME [authority], AMEN."

FOR ADDED BLESSINGS AND GROWTH

"...As he thinketh in his heart, *so* is he..." (Prov. 27:7)

This verse is one of the greatest PSYCHOLOGICAL and BIBLICAL PRINCIPLES.

WHAT A PERSON THINKS IS THE TYPE OF PERSON HE WILL MANIFEST:

- If one thinks negative worldly thoughts, then he WILL LIVE A NEGATIVE AND WORLDLY LIFE.

- If one TAKES INTO HIS MIND positive thoughts of faith, then HE WILL LIVE A POSITIVE LIFE OF FAITH.

- One CAN CHANGE A POOR SELF-IMAGE by developing good positive habits.

- One CAN STRENGTHEN ONESELF AND INCREASE FAITH by doing three things:

  1. Majoring on good, healthy thoughts,
  2. Washing ones mind by reading and memorizing scriptures, and
  3. Stating right objectives and positive goals

- ONE CAN DEVELOP A GOOD, HAPPY INNER SELF BY THIS SIMPLE DAILY EXERCISE.

A MUST!! REPEAT THE DAILY DECLARATIONS AT LEAST EVERY MORNING AND EVENING WITH MEMORIZATION BEING THE GOAL.

RETENTION, WILL IT BE 6% OR 62%

Do you want to learn? It is really up to you!!

These lessons were designed so you can maximize your ability to learn and remember what you read.

6 % — If you read an article once, chances are you will not remember much about it after a period of time. The average person can only recall 6% of what he read just two weeks earlier.

If, however, you read the article and review it for six consecutive days, your average retention goes up to 62%. **62 %**

To maximize your retention, the following method of study is given. On the first day, read your lesson for Monday and fill in Monday's blanks. On Tuesday, review Monday's questions before reading Tuesday's lesson and filling in Tuesday's blanks. On Wednesday, review the previous two days' questions before reading and filling in the blanks for Wednesday. Continue and do all lessons.

Each week when the Role Model comes to check your lesson, he will read each day's questions and when he comes to a blank, he will help you fill it in. After checking all the blanks, the Role Model will lead in a discussion of each day's principle.

When you finish the discussion of the week's exercises, you will have reviewed most of the principles six times, and your retention should grow to 62%

WILL IT BE 6% OR 62%

Lesson One

HOW TO HAVE SOMETHING IN HEAVEN WHEN YOU GET THERE

INTRODUCTION

MONDAY
"...he which soweth bountifully..."
(II Corinthians 9:6)

When billionaire Howard Hughes died, the common question was, "I wonder how much he left behind?" Thousands of column inches were given in speculation; radio and television commentators ran far and wide in their efforts to outguess the other experts on the question of how much Howard Hughes, the eccentric billionaire, left behind. Finally, an insignificant, smallish, baldheaded accountant, who worked on the staff of the controlling board of one of Mr. Hughes' high corporations, gave a startling, accurate answer to this question, when he said, "He left it all, every red cent of it. He never took one copperhead with him." Having read of the selfish, sinful, lustful life of Mr. Hughes for 35 years, I am sure that that answer was absolutely true. He left every red cent. He never took one copperhead with him ... but it didn't have to be that way.

Everyone has heard of someone who was spending money as though it were going out of style, and yet laughed at the cautioning of some parent, wife, or concerned person, and said, "You can't take it with you." But my friend: that is not true. One can take it with him.

Jesus commanded the Christian to lay up treasures in Heaven. This command would not have been given unless it was possible to lay up, or save one's treasures in Heaven. One CAN TAKE IT WITH HIM, or, to say it another way, one can send it on before him. Read the plain command from the lips of Jesus as found in Matthew 6:19-20.

"Lay not up for yourselves treasures upon earth, where moth and rust doth corrupt, and where thieves break through and steal: <u>But lay up for yourselves</u> [Who? For the preacher? For someone else? Nay, for yourselves.] <u>**treasures in heaven**</u> [that's for eternity], **where neither moth nor rust doth corrupt, and where thieves do not break through nor steal:" (+)**

A man with assets of twelve and one half million dollars was converted. He read that command – **"...lay up for yourselves treasures in heaven,.."** and thought within himself, "How can I convert all my holdings in oil, cattle, land, stocks and bonds into a treasure in Heaven?" He thought further, "Are cattle going to Heaven?" "No," was the answer. "Will oil go to heaven?" "No" was the answer. Then what goes to Heaven? Boys and girls, men and women go to Heaven. He then began to convert his physical holdings into cash and disperse the money into mission work, building church buildings, helping Bible colleges, and into every Christian work that would help get souls saved or prepare people for the work of the gospel.

Many years passed and a white haired old man smiled as he pressed his head to his dying pillow and said, "I did it!" "I did it!" "I have successfully converted all my oil, my cattle, and my stocks and bonds into spiritual dividends. All my earthly wealth has been converted into treasures in Heaven!" With that, he went to be with his treasures. He gave it to God. **(+)**

I. THERE ARE TWO OPTIONS FOR INVESTMENT

A. **This world's system.**

1. Jesus said, "you are in the world, but you are not of the world." **(+)**

2. "**...seek those things which are above,... ...Set your affection on things above, not on things on the earth... ...When Christ, who is our life, shall appear, then shall ye also appear with him in glory.**" [to be paid or rewarded for your work] (Colossians 3:1-4)

3. "**...be not conformed** [become like] **to this world: but be ye transformed by the renewing** [Studying the Bible to learn God's will and becoming more Christ like] **of your mind,..**" (Romans12:2) **(+)**

B. **The world and all that is in it will be destroyed.**

1. **Peter spoke of this event** in II Peter 3:10: "**...the Earth also and the works that are therein shall be burned up.**" **(+)**

2. **This age could end at any minute.** That's right. As these words are penned, there is no assurance that any new member will ever read them. Jesus MAY COME before your class is held. The Bible teaches that His coming is imminent. If He came tonight, the whole world system would go into the awesome great tribulation period. The world system would be destroyed.

C. **Which system are you going to invest in?**

1. **One system** declares that there is no danger of losing one's investment. There is no thief that will steal, and there is no loss of value due to wear or deterioration. The smallest investment will be remembered and rewarded; i.e., a cup of cold water.

2. **Another system** will not survive. All investments will be completely lost or destroyed.

3. **Which company would a financial expert recommend?** A growing company with a bright future or one that is doomed to bankruptcy and total loss. The Financial Expert who made both companies advises and commands: **"But lay up for yourselves treasures in heaven, where neither moth nor rust doth corrupt, and where thieves do not break through nor steal:"** (Matthew 6:20).

4. It is your money and your life! You have the power of decision. You will have to make the choice.

TUESDAY

II. PROSPERITY IS PROMISED TO THOSE WHO GIVE LIBERALLY

"Bring ye all the tithes into the storehouse, that there may be meat in mine house, and prove me now herewith, saith the Lord of hosts, <u>if I will not open you the windows</u> of heaven, and pour you out a blessing, that *there shall* not *be room* enough *to receive it.*" (Malachi 3:10) **(+)**

"Honour the LORD with thy substance, and with the firstfruits of all thine increase: <u>so shall thy barns be filled</u> with plenty, and thy <u>presses shall burst out</u> with new wine." (Proverbs 3:9-10) **(+)**

"The liberal soul shall <u>be made fat:</u> and he that watereth shall be <u>watered also himself.</u>" (Proverbs 11:25) **(+)**

"Give, and it shall be <u>given unto you;</u> good measure, pressed down, and shaken together, and running over, shall men give unto your bosom. **(+)** For with the same measure that ye mete withal its <u>shall be measured to you again.</u>" (Luke 6:38)

"But this I say, He which <u>soweth sparingly</u> shall reap also sparingly; and he which <u>soweth bountifully</u> shall reap also bountifully." (II Corinthians 9:6) **(+)**

   A. **God's Word promises financial prosperity.**

      If one would read these verses as he would a sales contract, or as he would a lease agreement, or as he would a legal, sworn document, he would believe. If he performed the first part of it, and met the first conditions, then he could claim the second part and expect the results promised.

B. **Read the Promises over again.**

"Bring ye all the tithes... I will pour you out a blessing and there will not be room enough to receive it." "Honour the Lord with thy substance..." "...first fruits..." "...barns shall be filled..." "...presses burst out..." "The liberal soul shall be made fat" "...he that watereth shall be watered..." "Give and it..." "...men shall give unto..." "...it shall be measured to you again."

We should face the Word of God honestly. God's Word promises financial prosperity to those who bring tithes and offerings. God not only gives financial prosperity to those who honor Him with their substance and with the first-fruits of their income, but He gives great peace and assurance to those who learn to make God a partner in material things. When one recognizes God's ownership of everything and gives tithes and offerings as a loving token of obedience, faith, and surrender, he enters into financial partnership with God. When this happens, he can claim the promise of Matthew 6:33, **"But seek ye first the kingdom of God, and his righteousness; and all these things shall be added unto you."** In the previous verses of the sixth chapter, Jesus illustrates how God takes care of the flowers and the birds that neither sow nor reap. He assures us that believers are much more important than flowers and birds. Then promises if ye seek first God, He will take care of and supply all your needs! The author claimed the promise of this verse in 1950, and God has literally supplied all his needs ever since. **(+)**

C. God's pay is good.

Matthew 19:27-29 shows that God will pay 100% interest on those investments. Think of what that means. 100% interest will be paid on the sacrificial decisions you make to follow the Lord and do HIS WILL! What a paycheck many will have at the judgment seat of Christ!

WEDNESDAY

III. THE TEMPTATION NOT TO GIVE LIBERALLY

The Devil works hard to prevent the Christian from giving to the Lord in a generous, systematic way. There are several methods with which he confronts the child of God in order to prevent him from giving. If he can stop his giving, he can stop his growing. If he can stop the Christian's giving (sowing) he can stop the Christian's reaping and rejoicing! The most God-like characteristic the Christian develops is giving. **(+)** The devil does not want the child of God to become GOD-LIKE. The Christian is commanded to be vigilant (watchful). He is to be watchful of his temptations in the realm of giving.

A. **Man's natural desire is to covet. (+)**

One does not have to teach a little boy to be selfish or to covet; it is his nature.

1. **Coveting is a respectable sin.** It is strange the way the sin of covetousness is considered by God's people. It is the respectable sin. It is the sin which strikes the deacon, the preacher, and the Sunday school teacher. The child of God who would never commit adultery, murder, or armed robbery thinks NOTHING OF COVETING.

2. **The sin of covetousness is best described as a Dr. Jekyl — Mr. Hyde sin.** To man it seems nice, acceptable, and a harmless practice. To God it is addicting, deferring from God's path, enslaving of one's will, alienating of one's love, and robbing of one's purpose.

3. **Coveting is a wicked sin.** Coveting is so dangerous, so wicked, so destructive to the individual, so dishonoring to God, that it is one of the sins of The Ten Commandments: "Thou shall not kill. Thou shall not commit adultery; Thou shall not covet...." Covetousness brought God's curse on Balaam (Numbers 22:21). Covetousness brought Leprosy upon Gehazi (II Kings 5:20). Aachan's Covetousness brought defeat to the army of Israel (Joshua 7) Covetousness brought death to Ananias and Sapphira (Acts 5:1-10), Covetousness is the sin of idolatry. (Colossians 3:5) **(+)**

The church at Corinth (I Corinthians 5:11) was commanded to withdraw from a brother and not to keep company with a brother if he be a fornicator, or covetous, or a drunkard, or an extortioner — no, not even to eat.

Coveting is behind all ungodly sin. The love of money causes all types of sin. (I Timothy 6:10)

For the love of money, the bar owner makes drunkards, paupers, and harlots out of people and damns their souls to hell. For the love of money, a woman sells her body. For the love of money, every type of sin is committed under Heaven. God hates this sin of coveting. **(+)** DO NOT be tempted to covet.

B. **The natural tendency is to walk by sight.**

Man loves to have faith as long as he can see where he is going. God commands tithing. He promises to bless and supply the needs of those who tithe, yet man has a problem believing or trusting God, because he:

1. **I can't tithe because of all these bills.** "I just can't see how we can pay our bills if we started tithing."

2. **We'll start tithing when things get better.** "When I get my bills paid down to where I can afford to tithe, I'd be happy to do it. I'll start then.

3. **I'm not going to give to that preacher.** There are many, who in looking for some

excuse to justify not giving to God, find fault with the preacher. The child of God is to WALK BY FAITH and TITHE BY FAITH. Do not be tempted to offend God by calling Him a liar through unbelief.

C. **A natural tendency to doubt.**

1. It won't do any good to tithe anyway.

2. That's what the old Jew said, **"It *is* vain to serve God: and what profit *is it* that we have kept his ordinance."** (Malachi 3:14) The subject under consideration in this passage is giving. They said, "It doesn't do any good to give anyway."

3. The farmer plants his crops, but he doesn't expect to reap them the next day or the next week. God's laws are sure, one will reap what he sows (It might take some time or be at a later date). DO NOT doubt God. Give Him the first fruit, and HE will give the harvest at the proper time.

    One can overcome the sin of coveting by tithing. Overcome the sin of doubting by giving liberally. Overcome walking by sight by tithing by faith. God's cure for a stingy-selfish-coveting spirit is to accept the promises of God literally and then give so He can honour His word by giving more back. **"Give, and it shall be given..."** (Luke 6:38) **"He which soweth sparingly shall reap also sparingly; and he which soweth bountifully shall reap also bountifully"**. (II Corinthians 9:6)

THURSDAY
IV. TITHING IS TAUGHT THROUGHOUT THE BIBLE

"And of all that thou shalt give me I will surely give the tenth unto thee." (Genesis 28:22)

"And all the tithe of the land, whether of the seed of the land, or of the fruit of the tree, is the LORD's: it is holy unto the Lord." (Leviticus 27:30)

The dictionary defines a tithe as: "To pay or give a tenth part of." In the Handy Dictionary of the Bible, Merrill C. Tenney, the following is said concerning the tithe: a tenth part of one's income set aside for a specific use **(+)**—to the government or ecclesiastics. Its origin is unknown, but it goes far beyond the time of Moses, and it was practiced in the lands from Babylonia to Rome. Abraham gave tithes to Melchizedek. (Genesis 14:20; Hebrews 7:2,6). Jacob promised tithes to God. (Genesis 2).

A. **Tithing was taught before the law.**

1. Ancient times. Most scholars believe that the language used concerning Abel demonstrated that he tithed. We know he brought offerings.

2. Abraham tithed. **(+)**

"And blessed be the most high God, which hath delivered thine enemies into thy hand. And he gave him tithes of all." (Genesis 14:20; see also Hebrews 7:2 and 6).

3. Jacob tithed 400 years before Moses lived.**(+)**

Jacob made a covenant with God saying, **"And this stone which I have set for a pillar shall be God's house, and of all that thou shalt give me, I will surely give a tenth unto thee."** (Genesis 28:22) **(+)**

B. **Tithing was incorporated into the law.**

1. All Israelites were commanded to tithe. (Leviticus 27:30-33)

2. The tithe was used to support the Levites and the temple service. (Numbers 18:21-32)

3. Additional tithes were required at times. (Deuteronomy 12:5-18; 14:22-29)

4. There were penalties charged for cheating on their tithes. (Leviticus 27:31)

5. The Pharisees tithed even on herbs: **"Woe unto you, scribes and Pharisees, hypocrites! for ye pay tithe of mint and anise and cummin, and have omitted the weightier *matters* of the law, judgment, mercy, and faith."** (Matthew 23:23)

6. The tithe in the Old Testament acknowledged and glorified God.

7. Every Christian should tithe. B. H. Hillard gave a summary of Malachi 3:8-12 as follows: **(+)**

   a. **Scriptural**: **(+)** "Bring <u>ye</u> all the tithe...." God has never relinquished His claim on the tithe as the minimum of one's gift.

b. **Simple: "Bring..."** (+)Yes, just as simple as coming to church and bringing the tithe; just as a parent brings a child. To "bring" implies complete control; coercive subjugation.
c. **Serviceable: (+) "...into the storehouse,.."** The church is God's storehouse, into which all the tithe is to be brought; none of which is diverted through extraneous channels.
d. **Sufficient: (+) "That there may be meat in mine house,.."** "Meat" means a sufficiency for every need; wherein, under any circumstances, the tithe did fail to meet the requirements, God will make provision for that which is lacking.

e. **Sublime: (+) "prove me now herewith,..."** "prove me..." means to give God a chance. To use a slang phrase, it means "to put God on the spot." It is accepting God's challenge. God yearns for a chance to bless His people; and that chance comes when we accept God's challenge.

f. **Sensible: (+) "If I will not open you the windows of heaven, and pour you out a blessing, that *there shall* not *be room* enough *to receive it*."** Common intelligence coupled with faith would lead one to tithe as the means of claiming such a promise. No person can believe this promise and fail to tithe. It would be unthinkable. Believe — tithe 10% Disbelieve -- fail to tithe. There is no alternative.

    g. Satisfying: **(+)** **"And all nations shall call you blessed, for ye shall be a delightsome land"** (Malachi 3:12).

C. **Jesus practiced tithing.**

1. He fulfilled the law. (Matthew 5:17-18)
2. He commended tithing. (Matthew 23:23; Luke 11:42) **(+)**
3. Jesus practiced what He preached.

D. **Paul taught that the New Testament ministry was to be supported in the same manner as was the Levitical ministry.**

FRIDAY
V. PAUL'S, TEACHING ON GIVING

    a. Does a soldier pay his own salary while in the army? (I Corinthians 9:7)

    b. Does a farmer plant grapes and not eat of the grapes? (Verse 7)

    c. Does a herdsman not partake of the flock? (Verse 7)

    d. Does an ox not eat of the corn? (Verse 9) **(+)**

1. **The spiritual realm of giving.**

He said that everyone who worked in a physical realm was a partaker of the fruit of his labor. Then, He applied the same principle to the spiritual realm. He stated in Verse 11, **"If we have sown unto you spiritual things, is it a great thing if we shall reap your carnal [material] things?"(+)**

2. **His illustration of supporting the ministry.**
   In verse 13, he asks them if they were not aware of how the Levites were supported. **"...They which wait [serve] at the alter are partakers with the alter?"** The Bible clearly teaches that the alter workers, temple workers, and priests were supported by the tithes and offerings of the Jewish people. **(+)**

3. **His statement on the standard of giving.**

   a. In verse 14, he begins with the expression, **"Even so."** This expression, **"Even so,"** comes from the Greek "Houtos Kai." This is the same word found in John 3:14: **"As Moses lifted up the serpent in the wilderness, even so [Houtos Kai] must the Son of man be lifted up."**

   b. "Houtos Kai" means in the same manner or in the manner previously described. **(+)**

   c. Paul's point is that the standard that was used of God to support the Old Testament priests and temple workers is the same standard he ordained to support **"...They who preach the** gospel..." That standard is **"Tithes and offerings."**

    d. The literal statement of verse 14 is **"Even so"** [Houtos Kai]. **"Even so hath the Lord ordained that they which preach the gospel should live** [to be cared for] **of the gospel"**

E. **"Let a man give as he purposeth in his heart."** (II Corinthians 9:7)

This is a fine standard to use when a person lets the Bible help him to set the standard.

    1. Paul was a Jew writing to a church (Church of Corinth), which was started in a Jewish synagogue and was made up of Jewish converts who were familiar with tithing. (Acts 18:7-8)

    2. The first example of a man purposing in his heart was Jacob. Jacob purposed to give back to God a tenth part or a tithe. (Genesis 28:22)

VI. GOD WANTS YOU TO GIVE OF YOUR LIFE SO HE CAN REWARD YOU DURING THE MILLENNIAL REIGN (ETERNITY)

A. The reason one should give to God is to express love and gratitude to God. God gave Jesus, His Son, health and all the material and spiritual blessings of life. One expresses his love and appreciation when he gives back to God.

B. Giving back to God is one of His methods, which causes spiritual growth in the believer. **"It is more blessed to give than to receive."**

C. One can have rewards waiting for himself in Heaven that will give him eternal blessings IF HE WILL GIVE TO GOD. **(+)** Let Him reward you and multiply you FOR IT.

D. **"...He which soweth bountifully shall reap also bountifully."** (II Corinthians 9:6)

DAILY DECLARATION
Repeat Aloud Each Morning And Evening

The promises of God concerning the blessings received from giving are just as true as all of His other promises.

MEMORY VERSE:

"Give, and it shall be given unto you; good measure, pressed down, and shaken together, and running over, shall men give into your bosom. For with the same measure that ye mete withal it shall be measured to you again." (Luke 6:38)

MY COMMITMENT

Having studied this lesson on giving, I now understand the reason God commands His children to give tithes and offerings. It is so that they may grow spiritually, and have treasures in Heaven when they get there. I now purpose in my heart to give liberally and systematically of my tithes and offerings. In doing this I will not only help support the work, which has greatly blessed me, but will follow the design plan of spiritual growth and of laying up treasures in Heaven.

CHECK BLOCK AFTER REPEATING

	Mon	Tues	Wed	Thurs	Fri	Sat	Sun
A.M.							
P.M.							

NAME:_____ GRADE:_____

Monday
(Introduction — Options for Investment)

1. **"Lay not up for yourselves treasures in _____ _____..."** (Matthew 6:19).
2. How did the millionaire convert his holdings into the spiritual dividends? _____ _____ _____ _____ _____.
3. You are in the world, but you are _____ of the _____ .
4. When Paul said, **"Be not conformed to this world"** (Romans 12:2), what did he mean? _____ _____.
5. Which system will not survive? _____ _____ (II Peter 3:10).

Tuesday
(Prosperity Promised)

1. What would a person have to do to secure the promise: **"Pour you out a blessing, that there .shall not be room enough *to* receive** _____ (Malachi 3:10).
2. What does God promise the person who will honour the Lord with his first fruits? _____ _____ _____ (Proverbs 3:9)
3. "The liberal soul shall be _____ _____ " (Proverbs 11:25)
4. **"Give, and it shall be** _____ _____ _____... ;shall men give into your bosom." (Luke 6:38)
5. He which soweth _____ shall reap _____, and he which soweth _____ shall reap also bountifully. (II Corinthians 9:6)

6. Are these promises of God literal or should we not believe them? They _____ _____.

Wednesday
(Temptation Not to Give)

1. The most God-like characteristics _____ _____ _____ _____ _____.
2. Man's natural desire is to _____.
3. What sin is the child of God most likely to commit? The sin of _____.
4. What sin caused the death of Achan, Ananias and Sapphira? _____ _____ _____ _____ _____.
5. What does God think of the sin of coveting? He _____ it.

Thursday
(Tithing is Taught)

1. What is the religious definition of "tithe"? _____ _____ _____ _____ _____ _____.
2. Was tithing taught before the law? Give an example. _____ _____.
3. Jacob gave tithes about _____ years before the law was given by Moses.
4. Give a Scripture, which commanded the Jews to tithe while under the Law of Moses. _____ _____ : _____.
5. Give the seven steps in Mr. Hillard's summary of Malachi 3:8-12.
   1. _____ 2. _____
   3. _____ 4. _____
   5. _____ 6. _____

6. Give the Scripture where Jesus commended tithing. _____ _____ : _____ and _____ _____ : _____
   7. _____

Friday
(Paul's Teaching on Giving)

1. Give an example that shows that one is to partake of the fruit of his labours. _____ _____.
2. Paul said, "if we have sown unto you spiritual things…we shall reap your _____ things?" (I Corinthians 9:11)
3. How were the Levites (temple workers) supported? By _____ and _____.
4. What does the expression "Houtos Kai" mean? _____ _____ _____.
5. God wants us to give liberally so we can _____ something when we _____ to _____.

Lesson Two
MY FIRST FAITH PROMISE MISSIONS CONFERENCE

INTRODUCTION
MONDAY

It wasn't difficult to trust the Lord and tithe when I became a Christian. I lived in a poor widow's home and witnessed how God had miraculously taken care of our family. **(+)**

It was not difficult to trust the Lord to take care of all my necessities **(+)** when I became a full time pastor. I never worked outside of the ministry except seven months while in Bible college for **the first thirty-five years** in the ministry. But to submit to the Lord in giving by faith **was one of the greatest struggles of my life. (+)**

There are several bits of information I want to give you before we get to the heart of my testimony.

First, I was saved on July 10, 1949, and requested the pastor to baptize me. He and a group of his members took me about one hundred yards out into the San Joaquin River near the mouth of the San Francisco Bay before we found water deep enough to baptize me. The bay is formed where the Sacramento and San Joaquin Rivers flow into the bay. Several months later, God preached me out of that church, and I knew that when I went down into the basement of the First Missionary Baptist Church in Brentwood, California, that I was home. I immediately requested membership in the church. The pastor, Ted R. Cooper, informed me that I would have to be baptized; I was not receptive to being immersed again. He took the

Bible and explained the reason for what I thought was his ridiculous request. My thoughts were, "Who are you? I'm almost wet from my last baptism."

But I had a problem! I knew that was where God wanted me to become a member. There was no doubt about it. So after arguing with the Lord in my heart for two or three months, I surrendered to the Lord (to **do anything he wanted me to do**) and consented to scriptural baptism. The date of my baptism was Tuesday, July 4, 1950. We had a workday in the morning on the new auditorium, a potluck dinner, then traveled twelve miles to Antioch, California, to use the baptistery of the First Missionary Baptist Church.

I was baptized and just twelve days later, on July 16, 1950, I was called to preach and **preached my first sermon that very night. (+)**

After twenty years of starting churches (five), pastoring, attending six years of Bible College (while pastoring and starting churches) and having earned three degrees (Th.G., Th.M. and Th.D.) in theology, I was pastor of the Landmark Baptist Church in Sacramento and president of Missionary Baptist College. I mention these facts to show you I was a seasoned, mature pastor and will HELP YOU understand the struggle I went through during our first faith promise meeting.

God had richly blessed me with a wonderful wife, Louella **(+)** (we were married forty-one and half years before she went on vacation to heaven) and five tremendous children.

MOST CHURCHES DID NOT TEACH TITHING

TUESDAY

In those days, many of the Missionary Baptist churches and pastors did not practice tithing **(+)** (much less Faith Promise). They were very intolerant toward other Baptist pastors and churches who were not Missionary Baptists. They believed we were in a great falling away period just before the second coming of Jesus and had become "guarders of the faith and inspectors of people's baptism." This led to a negative, intolerant attitude toward other Christians. **(+)** They were not missionary minded and only a very few preached and practiced personal door-to-door soul winning.

I loved their doctrinal views. However, in addition to just preaching on doctrine, I taught and practiced that children of God ought to become soul-winners. **(+)**

Just before I was called to become the pastor of the Landmark Baptist Church, the church was in an enlargement program to triple the size of their facility. A group had pressured the pastor to resign causing a split in the church. When I became pastor, the negative people were in control and ran the church. I threw myself into rebuilding the church membership and finishing the building program. I got the church to finance the completion of the facility by entering into a bond program that would furnish the money to finish the project. My family and I bought $2,000 worth of bonds on credit **to be paid off in twenty-four monthly payments.**

I took a mission trip to Mexico and met a tremendous Mexican preacher whom we could fully support for $80 US dollars a month. I knew it was God's will to adopt this man as our missionary and fully support him. The church agreed to allow us to do so only if people gave the money personally and not obligate the church in anyway. I got them to make this vote only on the condition that I, personally, **would pay any shortage of the $80 (+) out of my own pocket.**

The church was growing wonderfully with additions every week and one by one the people who had pressured the former pastor to resign all left. **But I still had a family of seven to support, pay church bonds, and had to make up the difference**, sometimes as much as one-half, of the $80 monthly missionary salary each month.(+)

DR. JACK BASKIN, A GREAT MISSIONARY AND PREACHER

WEDNESDAY

Dr. Jack, former missionary to Korea and Executive Vice-President of Pacific Coast Baptist Bible College and who had a great heart for missions, was our principle speaker in our first Faith Promise meeting. We had two or three missionaries come and show their slides. The church was giving ten percent of their income to missions, **(+)** but I knew God wanted us to do better.

A RIDICULOUS AMOUNT

As Dr. Jack encouraged us to begin to pray about how much God wanted us to give above our tithes and offerings, **God laid a ridiculous figure on my heart.** I thought, "God, that's dumb," **(+)** and dismissed it from my mind.

My First Faith Promise

Later, I prayed again and the same amount came into my mind. My thoughts were, "Devil, quit messing with my mind," and changed my prayer to other requests. **(+)**

Before I went to bed on Saturday night, the third day of our meeting, I tried praying about it a third time. The figure of **$20 a week** came into my mind again. My answer to God this time was a humble response, "$20 per week, Lord? That's almost twenty percent of what the church pays me **(+)** and with my wife, family, bond payments, and underwriting Ernesto's salary, there's no way. The only way I'll make it now is from the revivals I preach."

FOR THE NEXT THREE OR FOUR DAYS

The argument with God about the amount I should give continued in my thoughts for the next three or four days. It was there every time I tried to pray.

COMMITMENT TIME CAME

Dr. Jack handled that part of the service for me. After he explained that the Faith Promise offering was not the tithe. **Faith Promise is something that a person trusts God to do through him, something that he could not do by himself.**

I received my card and as he prayed... the $20 figure popped back into my mind.

I marked $10 per week down on my card and placed it face down into the offering plate.

Sunday night, Dr. Jack got up and while explaining Faith Promise – **it is something you trust God for** – the church will not bill you for it – it is between you and God. "Ushers, pass out the cards to those that didn't get one this morning." Then, he really got my attention. **It was like a command** – "you that God moved on your heart to give $20 a week that only marked $10, take another card and **mark $10 more**." **(+)** I very sheepishly complied with his command. "How did he know? My card was face down" I thought.

I STILL HADN'T SURRENDERED

THURSDAY

Though I complied by marking another card, I was not settled. A man named Harry interrupted my thoughts. Harry seemed to be a good man, but was living with Janet. **They were not married,** but I visited them in their apartment and they were genuinely saved and gave evidence of it by living a changed life. They were no longer living together and wanted to be baptized. I told them I would baptize them **after they were married**.

I WILL PAY THE PREACHER

Harry began by saying, "Wednesday night Pastor."

"What about Wednesday night, Harry?" I asked.

"That's when Janet and I want you to marry and baptize us," came his answer.

"Great," was my reply, "Do you have the license?" "Oh yes," was his answer. "All we've been waiting on **was enough money to pay the preacher." (+)**

"Pay the preacher?" was my reply. "You've been out of work since you broke your arm, besides I don't charge for weddings."

"You should," came his reply. "My dad always taught me, if you find a woman **worth marrying, she's worth paying for."**

I protested a little further but Harry was firm.

"I'm going to pay you. After all, you are the one who won us to the Lord and gave us happiness."

As I drove home that Sunday night, my family rejoiced over the blessings of the Lord. They were especially happy about Harry and Janet getting married. But I was still uncommitted about giving $20 a week to Faith Promise. **(+)**

My rebellious mind thought, since Harry is going to pay me for marrying him and Janet, **it will**

probably be $10 and that would be my Faith Promise offering. (+)

As I turned into our driveway, I was shocked at what I saw. On my front lawn was a sign about fourteen to sixteen inches high and ten to fifteen feet long. The sign had beautiful carved letters that spelled out "DR. JAMES WILKINS." **(+)** The letters were beautifully carved and painted white, they almost glowed when the headlights reflected on them. My whole family was totally amazed.

What had happened was an older man, a man whom I had led to the Lord, had carved the letters to show his appreciation for our family's kindness. He had been released from prison after serving twenty to twenty-five years. I met him and led him to the Lord. I let him stay on our property in a twenty-four foot trailer. We stocked the trailer with food for him as he waited for his son to come from back east and drive him home.

Wednesday night came and there was Harry and Janet all dressed up and waiting for me to marry them. We started the service with a song or two and then made the marriage part of the service. We concluded the service by baptizing them. **(+)** People broke into applause in their honor and a beautiful gift was presented to them.

GOD GAVE ME MY FIRST FAITH PROMISE OFFERING

FRIDAY

True to his word, Harry, with his hand stretched out. He was telling one of his friends, who came to witness their baptism and wedding. **"I've got to pay the preacher,"** and with that, he gave me the most crumpled piece of money I ever saw. You couldn't determine what size of bill it was because it had been folded so many times.

When I got back in the office, I unfolded it and just as I thought it would be, **it was a $20 bill. (+)** God seemed to have whispered into my ear – **I gave you your first week's Faith Promise offering**. It had to be the Lord, because $20 back then from a fellow who wasn't working was like $200 today. **For the first time**, I had peace in my heart concerning the amount of Faith Promise offering I should give.

My family got into our car and we drove the seven miles home. We lived in an old but well preserved home on top of a hill with a big lawn and yard. You could see the house regardless of the direction you were driving and there were hundreds of cars that passed right in front of our home every day. The sign, DR. JAMES WILKINS was very visible from both directions.(+)

A TIMID KNOCK

Since our friend still had three or four weeks before his son's arrival, we felt compelled to leave the sign up. Early the following week there was a timid knock on our door. I opened the door and a handsome young couple stood there.

The man asked, "Are you a reverend?"

"I'm a Baptist pastor," I responded.

"Do you do weddings?" he continued.

"I do, after I counsel with the ones getting married," was my answer.

They instantly broke into smiles and said, "We want that too. Will you marry us?"

"When?" I asked.

"Now," they answered, "We got our license."

"Come on in," I invited. I got my Bible and inquired about their spiritual condition. **Both were lost,** and I told them that the greatest way to insure a happy marriage was to accept Jesus as their Lord as well as their Savior. They both nodded their heads. I went into several principles including how to be saved.

They responded by accepting the Lord as their Savior.

This happened ten or twelve times over the next twelve months. Several were saved and baptized. Each time they would pay me in **with $20 bills. (+)**

THE SIGN BROUGHT OTHERS

There would be the same inquiry about whether I was a pastor or not.

"Yes," was always my answer.

"Do you do funerals? Mama died and lived in a rest home, or we are new here and we don't know a pastor – **BUT WE SAW YOUR SIGN**." They would always pay me in multiples of $20. **(+)** After performing a funeral or two for a certain funeral home, the director approached me by saying, "Pastor, I really like the way you do funerals. You are kind and helpful to the people. From time to time I need a preacher to do a funeral for me. Could I call you to help me?"

My answer was, "Yes, I'll be happy to assist in anyway I can." He always paid me (by check) in multiples of twenty dollars.

God was faithful in raising that $1,040 Faith Promise that year, and He did at times when I was available. He did it where it furthered my ministry because through the weddings and funerals several people joined our church.

I never dreamed that through my struggle of surrendering to Faith Promise that God would use it to encourage others to overcome their doubts and trust the Lord to bless them as he blessed me.

God made me into a perfect example of Faith Promise.

Faith Promise means to trust the Lord to do through you what you could not do yourself. (+)

When one surrenders and yields to Him to keep His promise – **life becomes a thrilling adventure.**

MY STORY IS AN ILLUSTRATION

The reason this complete story of my first faith promise conference is presented as a lesson is to **serve as an illustration to you**.

Not one word had been exaggerated. It all happened just the way I have penned it. In fact, I may have wrestled with my decision more than I was able to express in writing.

God does not need any human help to describe how He works in the lives of his children.

If you have been saved, then God is your father. He plainly states **that it gives Him pleasure to bless and help His children.**

He is **always present**. He is **all powerful**. He is **perfect in knowledge**, wisdom and grace. He has openly urged you to try (prove) Him so He can open the windows of heaven and bless you. (Mal 3:10-11)

Look at the flowers! – Ten's of thousands of varieties.

Look at the Birds! – They are all sizes and colors.

It will take Him **all eternity to reveal** what He has prepared for His children to enjoy. (Eph. 2:7) **He**

has unlimited numbers of ways to supply you with your faith promise offering. He is just waiting to show you how He will bring it to pass and fulfill the amount He has placed in your heart to give.

Many years after the weird way He brought my first faith promise money in, I am still amazed at how He works! How He honors the little faith which I exercise in Him. **He has given me my faith promise offering!**

…In many ways

From many sources…

He tests my faith at times by waiting **till the last moment** or even going a little past the time to give, **but He has never failed…**

AND HE WILL NEVER FAIL YOU

DAILY DECLARATION

Faith promise giving means to trust the Lord to do through you what you could not do for yourself.

MEMORY VERSE

By faith Enoch was translated that he should not see death; and was not found, because God had translated him: for before his translation he had this testimony, **that he pleased God**.

(Hebrews 11:5)

CHECK BLOCK AFTER REPEATING

	Mon	Tues	Wed	Thurs	Fri	Sat	Sun
A.M.							
P.M.							

MY COMMITMENT

Having studied this lesson on giving, I now understand that when God places an amount on my heart, He is more than able to supply the funds. I will look to Him to fulfill His promise and trust Him **so my faith will grow**.

NAME:_____ GRADE:_____

My First Faith Promise

INTRODUCTION
MONDAY

1. I witnessed how _____ had miraculously taken _____ of our family.
2. It was not _____ to trust the Lord to take care of all my _____.
3. But to _____ to the Lord in giving by faith **was one of the greatest** _____ **of my life.**
4. **I was called to** _____ **and preached my first** _____ **that very night.**
5. God had richly _____ me with a wonderful _____, Louella.

MOST CHURCHES DID NOT TEACH TITHING
TUESDAY

1. Many of the _____ Baptist churches and pastors did not practice _____.
2. This led to a _____ intolerance attitude toward other _____.
3. However in addition, to just _____ on doctrine I taught and _____ that children of God ought to _____ soul winners.
4. I got them to make this _____ only on the _____ that I, personally, **would pay any** _____ **of the $80.**
5. **Had to make up the** _____, **sometimes as much as** _____, **of the $80 monthly missionary salary each month.**

DR. JACK BASKIN,
A GREAT MISSIONARY AND PREACHER
WEDNESDAY

1. The _____ was giving ten percent of their _____ to missions.
2. **God laid a _____ figure on my heart.** I _____, 'God, that's dumb'.
3. My _____ were, 'Devil, quit messing with my mind' and _____ my prayer to other requests.
4. That's almost _____ percent of what the church _____ me.
5. "You that _____ moved on your heart to give $20 a _____ that only marked $10, take _____ card and **mark $10 more**."

I STILL HADN'T SURRENDERED
THURSDAY

1. "All we've been _____ on **was enough money to** _____ **the preacher**."
2. But I was still _____ about giving $20 a _____ to Faith Promise.
3. **It will probably be _____ and that will be my Faith Promise _____.**
4. The sign had beautiful _____ letters that _____ out "DR. JAMES WILKINS."
5. We _____ the service by _____ them.

GOD GAVE ME
MY FIRST FAITH PROMISE OFFERING
FRIDAY

1. I _____ it and just as I thought it would be, **it was a** _____ **bill**.

2. The _____, DR. JAMES WILKINS was very visible from both _____.

3. Each time they would _____ me in _____ **of $20 bills**
4. They would _____ pay me in _____ of $20.

5. **Faith** _____ **means to** _____ **the Lord to do through you what you could not do** _____

Lesson Three
HOW WOULD YOU LIKE TO HAVE JOY AND MULTIPLY YOUR INVESTMENTS?

INTRODUCTION
MONDAY

In order for us to comprehend the marvelous truths of this lesson, let me give a short scriptural foundation? I will deal with the marvelous truths of this lesson by answering five piercing questions.

Paul stated that God "was able to do exceeding abundantly above all that we ask or think according to the power that worketh in us." (Ephesians 3:20) Simply stated, God does things for his children that we never thought possible or ever entered into our minds. **(+)**

"A vision appeared to Paul in the night, in which a man of Macedonia stood and prayed, saying, come over into Macedonia, and help us." (Acts 16:9) Here we see God touching a man's heart that is in need, and Paul's heart at the same time and yet they were miles apart. **(+)**

We also have the statements concerning the omni-present Holy Spirit in Romans 8:26-27. This means that the Holy Spirit is everywhere at the same time as demonstrated by Paul's Macedonia call when The Holy Spirit moved on both their hearts while they were miles apart at the same instant. **(+)** This principle is also seen when the Holy Spirit worked on Peter's and Cornelius's hearts at the same time. "Likewise the Spirit also helpeth our infirmities: for we know not what we should pray for as we ought **(+)** but the Spirit itself maketh intercession for us with groanings which cannot be uttered. And he that searcheth the hearts knoweth what is the mind of the Spirit, because he maketh intercession for the saints according to the will of God. "**And he that searcheth the hearts knoweth what is the mind of the Spirit, because he maketh intercession for the saints according to the will of God.**" (Romans 8:26-27)

The passage of scripture that is the foundation of these unbelievable truths is II Corinthians 9:5-15. Now to our five questions.

QUESTION ONE
HOW WOULD YOU LIKE TO CAUSE SOMEONE TO BE, REALLY THANKFUL TO GOD?

In a world where most people are disappointed, heavy-hearted, and have very little hope, how would you like to cause them to lift their eyes toward heaven and really be thankful? You could change that spirit from one of uncertainty and doubt to that of thanksgiving to God.

YOU CAUSED IT! You are the one who made someone really thankful. **(+)**

QUESTION TWO
HOW WOULD YOU LIKE TO CAUSE SOMEONE TO PRAISE GOD?

God has given you every single blessing because **every good gift comes from above**. God so loved you that while you were yet a sinner, He gave His son to die for you on the cross. God allowed you to be born in this country, hear about salvation, and through the Holy Spirit, drew you to the Savior where you repented of your sins.

But there are other people in the world who are heavy-hearted and do not have any hope. How would you like to cause that person **to praise Jesus, who made everything in your life worthwhile?**

QUESTION THREE
HOW WOULD YOU LIKE TO FIND A WAY TO MULTIPLY YOUR MONEY?

Man, I'm sure that caught someone's attention! Multiply your money? That's what I said!

You say, that sounds like a fool's promise, a fool's game, a con artist's work.

Yes, I'm sure, humanly speaking, in this world where people do unto others before it is done unto them, and where all types of schemes are hatched up, it would be the natural reaction to doubt.

Let me ask you once again, how would you like to find a way to **multiply your money**, to multiply your investments? **There is a way.** I want to share it with you, but before I do, I want to ask two more questions.

QUESTION FOUR
HOW WOULD YOU LIKE PEOPLE TO REALLY APPRECIATE YOU, PRAY FOR YOUR WELL BEING, SUCCESS, AND HAPPINESS?

Does that sound like something you would really like to have happen in your life? Someone or better yet a group, may be praying for you, your happiness, success, and family. **Praying just for you?**

QUESTION FIVE
HOW WOULD YOU LIKE TO HAVE YOUR EVERY NEED MET?

Now, I didn't say **want**, I said need. How would you like to have your every need supplied? Would that be a tremendous way, regardless of how dark or uncertain things look or what is said about recession, inflation, or the trend to have a deep settled peace that you know that your needs will be met; your needs will be supplied?

THESE PROMISES ARE BASED ON THE WORD OF AN IMMUTABLE GOD

TUESDAY

God took an oath upon His own honor, upon His own word that He would perform these promises. It is as though you were in a courtroom and placed your hand upon the Bible and said, "I will not lie." Only God is saying, "I am in complete command of what I am saying, and I have absolute ability to bring it to pass."

Now, with that in mind, lets look at these tremendous promises once again.

1. How would you like to make someone thankful, to the level their whole disposition would change?

2. How would you like to cause the Lord who has been so good to you, receive **praise from other people.** God would receive praise for **something that you did**, by people that you have never known.

3. How would you like to have a return on the investment that you made which is multiplying? What you invest, or give, could multiply as much as a hundred fold. **(+)**

4. How would you like to have people that you have never seen or heard of you **pray for you sincerely**? People, who would lift up your needs to God and ask God to watch out, bless and help you?

5. How would you like to have the absolute assurance, regardless of what may come, that you would have your needs met?

Let us examine the scriptures found in II Corinthians 9:5-15 which make these promises. Paul is the author, humanly speaking, and is being directed by the Holy Spirit. Paul is writing a letter to the Church in Corinth. Let us begin at verse five.

Verse 5: "Therefore I thought it necessary to exhort the brethren, that they would go before unto you, and make up beforehand your bounty, [offerings] whereof ye had notice before, that the same might be ready, as a matter of bounty, and not as of covetousness."

Paul told the people and they agreed to take up an offering. He said the offering might be ready as a matter of bounty, and not of covetousness; otherwise it would be an offering rather than people being tempted to covet and hold what God had laid on their hearts to give.

Verse 6: "But this I say, He which soweth sparingly shall reap also sparingly; and he which soweth bountifully shall also reap bountifully."

In this verse Paul is stating a principle that is easy to understand. You sow a few stalks of corn and you reap a little corn but if one sows several acres of corn he will reap much, much corn. The application to spiritual things is also very simple. Invest or give a little to God and you will only have a little in the Bank of Heaven. Give a lot and have a lot in the Bank of Heaven.

Verse 7: "Every man according as he purposeth in his heart, so let him give, not grudgingly, or of necessity: for God loveth a cheerful giver."

The statement, "as he purposeth in his heart" means as he purposes to give to the cause of Christ.

Verse 8: "And God is able to make all grace abound toward you; that ye, always having all sufficiency in all things, may abound to every good work:"

This statement promises that if one gives liberally, as God wants him to, that God will supply all of his needs. **(+)**

Verse 9: "(As it is written, He hath dispersed abroad; he hath given to the poor: **his righteousness remaineth for ever."**

Verse 10: "**Now he that** ministereth seed to the **sower** both minister bread for your food, and multiply your seed sown, and increase the fruits of your righteousness;)"

Verse 11: "Being enriched in everything to all bountifulness, which causeth **through us thanksgiving to God.**" This very clearly states that what we give causes others to be thankful to God.

Verse 12: "For the administration of this service not only supplieth the want of the saints, but is abundant also by many **thanksgivings unto God.**" This verse confirms that "many" give thanksgiving to God for something we did.

Verse 13: "Whiles by the experiment of this ministration they **glorify God for your professed subjection unto the Gospel** of Christ, and for your liberal distribution unto them, and unto all men;" This verse adds, they not only are thankful, **but they praise God** because of what was done.

Verse 14: "And by their **prayer for you**, which long after you for the exceeding grace of God in you." This verse states that they begin a process of praying for you.

Verse 15: "Thanks be unto God for his unspeakable gift."

Now please note that all of these promised blessings come from an **act that you can do.**. You can give your offering to God. This offering will be given to a missionary that needs help in establishing his church in order to reach out to the lost world.

- Sent to needy people who need to hear the Gospel
- Sent to needy people who need food and clothing
- Sent to a missionary who is establishing a church which will reach out to the Lost

Let's take the five promises in order and examine each one of them more fully.

THE FIRST PROMISE IS YOU CAN MAKE SOMEONE THANKFUL TO GOD.

In these verses we have the example that illustrates **the needs we have in the desperate, dark world, which surrounds us;** poor people in a famine situation caused by severe drought. Paul has challenged the churches to respond to their needs by giving a liberal sacrificial offering.

Their needs caused **their desperate cry to God**.

God responds to their cries by moving on the hearts of his people to help. **(+)**

When people receive this help, through God's work, "...which causeth **through us thanksgiving to God.**" (verse 11); This thanksgiving to God was caused by God's people giving to meet their needs.

Examine The Needs of Our Lost World

All over the world we have people who are very poor and **have no hope** because they are held captive by false religion. **They are scared**; they live a life that brings them very little comfort, hope or peace. They have been kicked and tossed about, and it seems **they only have a dismal future**. In this desperate condition, their hearts cry out to God.

He looks down and sees their loneliness, their needs, their tears, and their futile condition of facing death and hell **without any hope**.

God moves on your heart, which causes you to give liberally to God.

God in turn **takes that gift, through a missionary**, to those people who may be halfway around the world.

The missionary gives the message to them which fills their need as expressed in verse 11, "Being enriched in everything to all bountifulness, which **causeth through us thanksgiving to God."**

Can you envision the little one, when he opens that package of food, or someone who lives in paganism, **hears** of the love of God? Their hearts are opened and they call upon the name of the Lord. Then the peace, joy and happiness of receiving Christ as their Savior comes flooding into their soul. The sin, the doubt, and hopelessness is gone. They weep because of their thanksgiving and **it was caused by you**.

Look again, please, in verse 12; not only supply the want of the saints, but supply in abundance, "**by many thanksgivings unto God."** In other words, here they are; they want a church building so badly but they are so poor and the cost is so high. Inflation in many foreign countries is a thousand times what it was a few years ago. If they go to church they stand **under a tree** as the blistering sun beats down upon them; or the chilling, threatening arctic wind pierces **through their light clothing**. But now, **through your liberal giving**, they can sit inside their own church building. They won't have to be open to stares and insults and the persecution of some passerby. They have pride and identity, as they open their hearts in praise toward God. You are the reason for that joy, that victory and thanksgiving! IT IS **BECAUSE YOU GAVE! (+)**

Pay attention to this point. In heaven **you come to God's attention NOT because of your prayers or needs**. You come to God's attention in heaven because there are people crying out to God in thanksgiving **BECAUSE YOU GAVE.**

THE SECOND PROMISE
YOU CAUSED SOME PEOPLE TO PRAISE YOUR WONDERFUL SAVIOR

Wouldn't it be great to live knowing, regardless of how hard pressed we become, how busy we get, how distracted we are, that as a Christian, **we are causing Jesus to receive praise?**

In verse 13, it states, "**they glorify God for your professed subjection** unto the Gospel of Christ and **for your liberal distribution unto them and unto all men.**"

As a Christian, we strongly believe the Gospel. We are convicted that unless the Gospel (death, burial and resurrection) is preached and people accept Jesus as their Savior, they are lost and will go to hell.

Some of those lost people live thousands of miles away.

Someone must carry the Gospel to him or her. That means money for passage to their land. Someone must learn the language and while they are in "language school", they must support their family.

God has moved on hearts and they have subjected to the Gospel by surrendering to go. They obeyed the wooing of the Holy Spirit.

Back home still other Christians have to be subjected themselves to the Gospel. God burdens their hearts to give liberally and systematically.

The gift is given to them through the missionary. As a result **they are born of God**, they become God's children. They begin to praise and glorify God. This happens because of your simple giving, your subjection to the Gospel, your humbleness, your submitting, your willingness to do what God laid on your heart to do, sacrificially.

ANSWER THE FOLLOWING QUESTIONS

Do you really want to praise Jesus?
Has He saved you from hell?
Has He given you a good home, a good wife/husband, a good family?
Has He given you precious people who pray for you?
Has He given you health, comfort, plenty to eat, and a good pastor?

Then here is a way that you can get people **to glorify and praise the Lord who has given you all these blessings.**

The simple act is giving!

In heaven you will come to God's attention, not because of your prayers or needs. You will come to God's attention because there are people praising him and **you caused their praise** BY GIVING! **(+)**

THE THIRD PROMISE
HOW TO MULTIPLY YOUR INVESTMENTS

WEDNESDAY

How would you like to find a way to multiply your investments, your money?

I didn't say a safe investment in which you will not lose your investment.

My question to you is, how would you like to find a way so that **your investment will multiply?**

Please examine the verse that makes this absolute promise; "Now he that ministers seed," that's the preacher or missionary. In this verse, you will find that the seed is you (who gave), the seed is your money, and the seed is your investment.

In Matthew 13, the Bible tells of a sower (preacher) who sows the seed which is the Word of God or the message.

That is exactly what you are doing, you are making it possible for him to go and sow by giving him the tools. You are a co-laborer with him by your faithful giving. **(+)**

Notice the wording in this verse. It says, "Minister bread for your food and multiply the seed sown."

In this statement, we have a double barrel promise.

First, there is a promise that you will be fed, **bread for your food.**

Second, you will multiply your seed (money) sown or given.

You give sacrificially, $20 to $25 per week or maybe it is $50 or $100. I know people who equal their car payment or more **in their Faith Promise giving.**

It will not be not easy for you to give solely by faith at first. You will have to stay humble and focused in order to do it. Sometimes it doesn't come in and you go ahead and give it anyway.

That money goes **to your partner, the missionary**, who is the one who is giving out the seed, the Gospel of hope.

The seed falls into a good and honest heart that believes and gets saved. The person who got saved **has 50-100 family members and a ton of friends.** Within two or three years many of them get saved. One of them becomes a great preacher who wins thousands. **Your seed is multiplying and has begun to produce much fruit!**

It was your humbleness in giving, your subjection to the Gospel of Christ that caused you to give.

Paul spoke of the members of the Philippian church who gave or **invested their money in him**. They were the only people who supported Paul. They gave to his necessities, his real needs. He couldn't have kept going without their sacrificial giving.

Paul was a tough guy who worked through pain and persecution. When he uses the word **afflictions**, it must have been hard work, something very difficult.

But notice Paul's response to the difficulties. He said concerning their giving, "**not that I desired a gift [or your money] but I desire fruit that would abound to your account.**" (Philippians 4:17)

Now think about those words dear friend. Paul went and won souls and **the support of the Philippians made it possible for him to do so.**

They invested in Paul and Paul won thousands to Christ and he said that those he had won **abounded to their account**. That is so thrilling to me and it gives you, the member, a tremendous **opportunity to earn or share in great rewards. (+)**

THE MULTI-LEVEL PRINCIPLE

Most people in America have been introduced to different multi-level companies. Many of those companies are headed by people who seem to be self-seeking and self-serving. They have soured people to the multi-level concept by their dishonest and questionable practices. Regardless of their poor image and impression of the multi-level concept, **the Bible teaches that much of God's system of rewards is based upon the multi-level principles.**

Let me briefly explain this concept to those who may not be clear on what we are talking about?

A person gets into a multi-level business under a sponsor. He is in what is called his first generation, which means that **every time he sells some of the company's product he receives a percentage of the commission** as a payment.

He recruits other people into the business, which **becomes the sponsor's second generation** and he gets a percentage of their commission as a payment.

These people (second generation) hire other people into the business, **which becomes the sponsor's third generation**. This means he receives a commission on every thing they sell.

The same principle is true concerning the fourth, fifth, sixth and on and on generation.

THE PHILIPPIAN CHURCH WAS PAUL'S SPONSOR

Paul, writing to the Philippian church, said "that's what I am writing about. I went down there and you sponsored me."

God gave me thousands of converts.

I started several churches.

I had several men become good preachers and they started other churches.

And you, the church (sponsor) over-wrote it all.

You get a portion and a percentage of the credit of all souls saved and churches started.

I am talking about an investment that really multiplied.

I'm talking about giving --- **giving that multiplies. (+)**

THE SOWER IN MATTHEW THIRTEEN

Some of the Gospel seed fell into good ground (good hearts), people who won and had a down line that returned thirty fold – which is 3,000 percent growth.

Some of the Gospel seed that fell into good and honest hearts grew to sixty fold or 6,000 percent growth.

Some of the Gospel seed that was sown returned a staggering one hundred fold or 10,000 percent. **(+)**

Remember, Paul announced that God was able to do abundantly more than we could imagine or visualize.

Visualize the following illustration that explains what Paul told the church, not that I desire a gift [your money]; but I desire fruit that may abound to your account."

Plant one seed of corn, the seed germinates (dies) and comes up a beautiful stalk of corn with one ear of corn **that has three hundred kernels of corn**. You shell out the corn and plant **300 seeds of corn** the following spring. Each seed germinates (dies) and produces **300 stalks of corn** with each stalk producing one ear which has **300 kernels of corn**. That is the way that the Gospel seed abounded in human hearts that were sown by the apostle Paul. (I Cor 15:36)

This illustrates the tremendous potential of those that give liberally to spread the Gospel to a lost and dying world. **(+)**

QUESTION FOUR
HOW WOULD YOU LIKE FOR PEOPLE TO "REALLY" PRAY FOR YOU?

THURSDAY

At times it seems as if no one really cares. You look to your family and they are busy. Then you go to your parents and find they too are busy. The preacher is preoccupied and as you look around it seems that you are all alone.

You have a need. To you, it is a real problem. There is something in your life that is serious and you don't know where to go, where to turn.

You become a little bit aggravated, a little bit let down, and no one seems to care.

In that situation, how would you like for someone to **"really" pray for you**? **(+)**

This is what the word of God states in verse fourteen, "**and by their prayers for you.**"

God is the one who stated that He promised that they would pray for you. "The immutable, unchangeable, unalterable God who cannot lie, and who took an oath that he would not lie, and promised **that someone would pray for you.**

Imagine this, here you are in a crisis **and somewhere** else people are in a worship service. A woman in a worship service looks around and sees her husband and her children. Her children are clean-cut and their eyes are glowing. They are happy and obedient. Sitting beside her is her faithful husband, which makes her feel secure.

She thinks, "**Where did this security and happiness come from**? It started when we became Christians, when our family got saved." All of a sudden there came a spirit of gratefulness and gratitude to God that He placed into her heart and now the Holy Spirit takes over. He caused her, in that far off land, to **think about the one or ones** who brought this happiness into her life.

Then God burdens her heart to pray for you in **the very moment of your crisis. (+)**

There in that distant place she begins to pray to God. "Oh God, **that person who gave their monies so that the missionary could come** – Bless that person, Father --- help them --- please."

In her heart, she thinks "Our family was saved four years ago --- what a change from the drunkenness – from the futility in our lives --- what a change in our children – It is all because the Gospel came to us --- Oh, dear Lord, bless that person who gave that which enabled the missionary to come and win us to the Lord. **It has so changed our lives**."

So God moves on others who live in that area to pray --- a bedridden saint who has been reached through **your liberal giving** --- with tears in her eyes --- begins to pray for you. On down the way the Holy Spirit moves on another and then another of his children **to pray for you. (+)** That bedridden saint who is in constant pain as she faces death, with an absolute hope of heaven, thanks God for **your liberal giving which brought hope and assurance instead of fear and darkness**. With her mind, now, forever focused on heaven, the Holy Spirit moves on her heart **--- TO PRAY FOR YOU.**

Consider the illustration of God leading the household of Cornelius who was lost. God **begins to deal with them** about their sins **while at the same time** directing Peter to go and give them the Gospel.

God works in **the same way by directing people to pray for the ones that help bring the Gospel to them**. The person or persons have a sense (placed there by the Holy Spirit) that something is wrong somewhere… "Oh, God be with that one, whoever it is and whatever it is – Oh, God help them… deliver them."

You are in a crisis and it seems that nobody cares. Suddenly the Holy Spirit reassures you of what's right. He relieves your burden and YOU MAKE THE RIGHT DECISION. You will never know why you were protected from the dangers, from the horrible ordeal until you get to heaven.

It is all because you gave sacrificially. Your gift went out there and changed lives and then they, in thanksgiving, grew close to God and were moved by the Holy Spirit to "really" pray for you.

God laid it on their hearts because "The Holy Spirit helpeth us with our intercessions because we do not know how to pray." In that distant land he helps those people to pray for you. God hears that prayer and delivers you from your crisis or needs.

This scripture (vs. 14) explains why I received a very unusual note from a close preacher friend a few years ago when our church was going through a crisis.

It read: **"Bro. Jim, I had this uncontrollable urge to pray for you. I suddenly broke out in tears** and sobbed out, 'God, help Brother Jim.' Then I felt like everything was ok."

What causes the chain reaction to occur?

It is because you **gave liberally!**

THANK GOD FOR HIS UNSPEAKABLE GIFT.

QUESTION FIVE
HOW WOULD YOU LIKE YOUR EVERY NEED TO BE MET?

The fifth promise is your needs will be met.

The Bible promises, "But seek first the kingdom of God and His righteousness and all these things will be added unto you." (Matthew 6:33)

When I first discovered that verse, I thought, "All things will be added unto me, WOW! What an all encompassing promise, ALL THINGS!"

"What things?"

I looked back to the previous verses that directed me, "Look at the sparrows." The words declared, "they don't sow, they don't reap; but God feeds the sparrows."

Then the question is asked, "Aren't you more important than the sparrows?" I deduced that those words meant; if God feeds the birds then He would take care of supplying me with food.

I read a little further in the scriptures and it said, "Look at the lilies, even Solomon, who perhaps was the greatest dresser and had the richest attires of anyone that ever lived, is not clothed as beautifully as the flowers." Then we have this declaration, "Wherefore, if God so clothe the grass of the field, which today is, and tomorrow is cast into the oven, shall he not much more clothe you, O ye of little faith?" (Matthew 6:30)

God impressed upon me, when I was a young man, that this verse meant: if I would put God first, His righteousness and his kingdom, and then really pray and say, "God give me a tender heart to be under subjection to the Gospel and do what you want me to do. Help me be a faithful steward and give the monies you place in my hands to give to others then, you will take care of all my needs."

It is reasonable to believe that if God feeds the sparrows and clothes the lilies then he will certainly take care of you. **(+)**
Examine God's great and bountiful promise to you in **verse eight**.

God is **able** to make **all** grace abound toward you; that ye, **always** having **all** sufficiently in **all** things, may abound to every **[all]** good work.

Please note the all-inclusive word, **ALL**.

Regardless of how America is doing, whether we have inflation, whether we have recession, whether you lose your job, whether you lose your health, or regardless of what happens to you, who give liberally, you have God's all consuming promise.

God has not only promised, but He is looking forward to supplying all your needs.

He has the ability to do so. He never slumbers. He is always available, in all things, to all good works, and **it is all because you believed His word and gave. (+)**

Through your giving you caused people **to be thankful**, their hopeless need was met, and their lives were changed.

You not only caused them to be thankful but **you caused them** to praise God! The one who gave His son for you, the one who keeps you alive. The one who touched your heart ... They're praising Him on your behalf because you were under subjection (submitted) to the Gospel which means you obeyed what the Bible said, **"and gave liberally!"**

Not only that, but your seed is multiplying. More people are getting saved.

More people are working for the Lord.

More people are praising and thanking God.

More people are praying for you.

You can have more assurance that your needs will be met and **you will have all sufficiently...always.**

BOTH ARE CHANNELS OF BLESSINGS

FRIDAY

You are a channel. God wants to **bless the world through you** and then reverse the blessing

Have Joy and Multiply your investments

from those that you blessed so **they can channel blessings back to you. Only God could do that!**

God looks down longing to find someone that He can do that with and for. **(+)**

Take an inventory by asking some questions.

How much of the money you make, are you keeping?

Just how well off are you?

Are you one of those who just makes it from paycheck to paycheck?

Do you run out of money before you run out of month?

Are you among those who are broke by the twenty-seventh of the month?

Is that an exciting way to live?

Do you say, Hallelujah! I'm broke again?

Is it fun when you don't have any lunch money for the kids and the possibility is it may get worse instead of better?

If that isn't a wonderful way to live and you don't enjoy it, why don't you consider doing something else?

CONSIDER SOME OF THE THINGS THAT CAUSE THOSE PROBLEMS

Often times the car is running well but on an impulse you go down and trade it in on a new one. Just driving it off the lot **you lose thousands** of dollars. You also extend your car payments and get in an upside down position with higher payments. When you stop to think about it, **in the light of eternity,** it wasn't a very smart decision. **(+)** If you had kept the older car, you probably could have squeezed out $50 to $100 to invest in missions.

You really don't have to buy those kids designer jeans, especially on your credit card. Compare the price of plain jeans with designer jeans. If the kids want them badly enough, **have them save up their money** and pay the difference. The same goes for shoes or toys or other items that you think you must have.

When you live your life in the light of eternity, in the light of what the Bible teaches, **you would soon incur God's favor**, both in the lives of your children as well as in your own life.

The Bible commands, "be not conformed to the world [its styles and way of thinking] but be ye transformed by the **renewing of your mind** that you might prove what is that **good, perfect and acceptable will of God**. "God is stating – prayerfully consider the decisions you make, the things you buy in the light of the word of God and eternity, and you will find that good and perfect will of God.

By tightening your belt, making a budget, and prayerfully working at following and pleasing God instead of living like a lost person in **the world, you could soon be making** a liberal, consistent offering to missions.

Soon you would be responsible for people you have never met, who **would be praising and giving thanks to God,** because they now have peace in their hearts and purpose in their lives.

Because of you, they would be **praising God,** and God would become so mindful of you **because of something you did (and are doing).**

You were under subjection (obedience) to the Gospel. In addition to that, you would be making an investment. An investment which has the potential of returning one hundred fold – that is a staggering **10,000 percent increase.** WOW! Not only that, but the Bible states it is an everlasting inheritance that will befit a person in ages to come.

Instead of moving into a larger house, rearrange the old one. Keep the old car. If you really want to, you can start making a bigger investment. You can lay up treasures in heaven, which will put you in a big house for 1,000 years **(+)** in the Millennium. **You can find the money!** When you do and you face a depression or a problem, instead of going to the counselors at $50 to $100 an hour for months, the people you helped **will pray for you**. The difference between victory or defeat **is prayer**.

God becomes your umbrella of protection. You are sheltered from sickness and doctor bills. You don't feel the pressure so y**ou are not as irritated with your wife or family**. You do not cause them irritation, which causes them to go on a spending binge. You will not get so up tight that you just have to "**get away**." When you have to get away, the expenses generally go on that credit card with high interest. After the "get away" you come back home to the same old problems. (+)

No, you can have peace of mind, hope, joy, and a home of love because of God. The number one thing that you need is to have someone to love you, to understand you, to help you and be your friend.

God has designed a life just like that for you.

One, you can make people really thankful to God **by giving**.

Two, you will cause someone to praise your blessed Savior **by giving**.

Three, you will multiply your investments **through giving**.

Four, you will have people pray for you, your success, and for your happiness, which will transform both you and your investment.

Five, you will have your every need met. Look around you. Take inventory of the people who have about the **same problems you do** that seem to be peaceful and successful. **Who are they? They are the givers.**

These are promises that God makes to His children who sacrifice to get the Gospel to a lost and dying world.

You are a channel of blessings to them and **God makes them a channel of blessings to you. (+)**

THANKS BE UNTO GOD FOR HIS UNSPEAKABLE GIFT
Introduction
MONDAY

1. Simply stated, _____ does things for his _____ that we never thought _____ or ever entered into our minds.
2. Here we see God _____ a man's heart that is in need and Paul's _____ at the same time.
3. The Holy Spirit moved on both their _____ while they were miles _____ at the same _____.
4. Likewise the Spirit also _____ our infirmities: for we know not what we should _____ for as we ought:
5. **YOU** _____ **IT!** You are the one who made someone really _____.

THESE PROMISES ARE BASED ON THE WORD OF AN IMMUTABLE GOD
TUESDAY

1. What you _____, or give, could _____ as much as a _____ fold.
2. This statement promises that if one gives _____, as God wants him to, that God will _____ all of his _____.
3. **God** _____ **to their cries by moving on the** _____ of his people to help.
4. You are the _____ for that joy, that victory and _____! IT IS **BECAUSE YOU** _____!
5. You will come to God's _____ because there are people _____ him and **you caused their praise** BY _____!

THE THIRD PROMISE
HOW TO MULTIPLY YOUR INVESTMENTS
WEDNESDAY

1. You are a _____ with him by your _____ giving.
2. It gives _____, the member, a tremendous _____ **to earn or _____ in great rewards**.
3. I'm talking about _____ --- **giving that _____**
4. Some of the Gospel _____ that was sown returned a _____ one hundred fold or _____ percent.
5. This illustrates the tremendous _____ of those that _____ liberally to spread the _____ to a lost and dying world.

HOW WOULD YOU LIKE FOR PEOPLE TO "REALLY" PRAY FOR YOU?
THURSDAY

1. In that _____, how would you like for someone to "really" _____ for you?
2. Then God _____ her heart to pray for you in **the very _____ of your _____**.
3. On down the way the Holy Spirit move on _____ and then another of his children **to _____ for you**.
4. It is reasonable to _____ that if God _____ the sparrows and clothes the lilies then he will _____ take care of you.
5. He is always _____, in all things, to all good _____, and **it is all because you _____ His word and gave**.

BOTH ARE CHANNELS OF BLESSINGS
FRIDAY

1. God looks down _____ to find _____ that He can do that with and for.
2. When you _____ to think about it, **in the light of** _____, it wasn't a very _____ decision.
3. You can lay up _____ in _____, which will put you in a big house for 1,000 _____
4. After the "get _____" you come back home to the _____ old _____.
5. You are a _____ of _____ to them and God makes them a channel of _____ to you.

DAILY DECLARATION

In my short journey on earth, I will be joyful as I strive to lay up treasures in heaven by investing in world missions.

MEMORY VERSE

And now, brethren, I commend you to God, and to the word of his grace, which is able to build you up, and to give you an inheritance among all them which are sanctified. Acts 20:32

CHECK BLOCK AFTER REPEATING

	Mon	Tues	Wed	Thurs	Fri	Sat	Sun
A.M.							
P.M.							

MY COMMITMENT

I will accept my place in world missions by witnessing to those in my personal world and investing by faith in the lives of missionaries both in the United States and in the uttermost parts of the world.

NAME: _____ **GRADE:** _____

LESSON FOUR

YOUR FINANCIAL OBLIGATION TO GIVE UNDER THE GREAT COMMISSION

INTRODUCTION
MONDAY

In Romans 10:13, Paul boldly states the great news that **"Whosoever shall call upon the name of the Lord shall be saved." (+)** As a missionary, he penned the questions which reveal our personal and financial obligation within the Great Commission. **(+)**

He asked:
- "How then shall they call on Him whom they have not believed?"
- "How shall they believe on Him whom they have not heard?"
- "How shall they hear without a preacher (messenger)?"
- "How shall they preach except they be sent?" **(+)**

In this one wonderful statement and four heart searching questions God spotlights the fearful responsibility of **every member of the local church. (+)**

LEARN THIS LESSON EARLY IN LIFE

As we journey through this life.
From the cradle to the grave.
The part of life one gives
Is the only part **that is saved! (+)**

I. **FINANCIAL OBLIGATION VIEWED AS A RESPONSIBILITY**

TUESDAY

A. **RESPONSIBILITY TO BE SHARED BY ALL**

Jesus gave the Great Commission to His church of saved, baptized believers. In order to come to your personal obligation under this age long commission please consider three negatives and one positive declaration.

1. **The Commission wasn't given just to preachers. (+)** Preachers are part of the local body of Christ and as such must bear responsibility of getting the gospel to the lost world. But the commission does not place them under any more responsibility than it does any other saved person.
2. **The Commission wasn't given to just the called.** The Bible teaches that God calls men into the mission field. (Acts 13:1-3). This special call does not supersede the command of Jesus which is found in the Great Commission. It identifies their particular field of labor and purpose, but it does not add more responsibility than what they already had.
3. **The Commission wasn't given to just the gifted.** Many seem to think that if one has the means then he can give to missions. Somehow, in their thinking, there are levels of responsibility to missions. **Preachers, deacons, and those that can afford to give have a responsibility, but many who are not "gifted" are excused.** This is false thinking *which was* forever dispelled by the story of the widow who gave her mites to the

Lord. "For unto whomsoever much is given, of him shall be much required." (Luke 12:48) This is true, but it does not NULLIFY the obligation placed upon all by the Great Commission.

4. **The Commission was given to all members.** In Romans 1:14, Paul stated the personal responsibility of every believer when he wrote; "**I am debtor** both to the **Greek** and to the **Barbarians**, both to the **wise** and to the **unwise**."

B. **RESPONSIBILITY IS TO BE SHARED EQUALLY**

1. **The missionary and his family give all.** (+) They sell their home, give up their treasurers, personal items, say goodbye to loved ones and friends and go to an uncertain place of service. **Much sacrifice and human denial goes into their decision.** Stop and personalize their decision by visualizing the faces of your children or grandchildren on the face, of the next missionary who visits your church. **Missionaries give all!**

2. **The informed give** money. It is amazing at the percentage of money that many in local churches give to the Lord. It seems that the more a person learns about the Bible and by faith follows it's teaching, **the more he abounds in his giving**. But most Christians limit their obedience to the Great Commission by giving money. When they give, it seems that **they feel like** they fulfilled their responsibility to the commission.

3. **The average member gives little.** Many give a waitress a bigger tip than they give to missions. **(+)**

4. **"But by an equality."** The inspired word states that every believer is under the **same obligation**. In his second letter to the Corinthian church, Paul said that God didn't intend for some to be **burdened while others are at ease** (doing nothing) "but by an **equality**." (II Cor. 8:13-14) God does not require some to give all, others give money and the rest give nothing. This unscriptural practice causes harm, discouragement and failure in the Lord's work. The Bible teaches an equal responsibility under the Great Commission. **(+)**

C. RESPONSIBILITY TO GIVE PRAYERS, ENCOURAGEMENT AS WELL AS FINANCIAL SUPPORT.

If all of our members gave financial support to missionaries, it would bring revival. Imagine what could happen if we begin to get involved by:

1. **Becoming acquainted with our missionaries.** A church could become acquainted with our missionaries and their families by developing an informational booklet. In **this** booklet we would place the name, age, hobby, and photograph of each member of the **family**. There could be testimonies with other personal information about their backgrounds. A church could have a reception for the **family** where each member of the family was recognized and awarded. Many members testify that they had a life changing experience when a missionary and his family were guests in their home.
2. **Becoming informed.** In addition to special services, the letters of missionaries can be

posted on the Mission Board. Portions of letters could be read before Sunday School classes or services.
3. **Becoming involved.** Special prayer meetings could be held regarding missionaries and their needs. Gifts could be donated and sent to missionaries and their families on special occasions. **The focus of the church should be on our business. The church's business is Missions.** (+) As part of the local church family, it is your obligation to get involved in prayer for, in the encouragement of, as well as in the financial support of our missionaries.

II. **FINANCIAL OBLIGATION VIEWED AS AN EXERCISE OF FAITH**

WEDNESDAY
A. **COMMANDED TO GROW IN GRACE AND IN KNOWLEDGE.**
The Apostle Peter was the first, and perhaps the most successful pastor God ever chose. It was under his human leadership that the Holy Spirit performed the works recorded in the first eight Chapters of Acts. The last words of this great pastor should be considered as among the most important words found in the Bible. His last words were, "But **Grow in Grace** and in the **knowledge** of our Lord Jesus Christ." (II Peter 3:18) **(+)**
1. **The natural laws of growth.** As soon as a healthy baby is born he begins to grow. This principle is true in the spiritual realm also. **The baby must have both food and exercise** in order to develop into a healthy normal child.
2. **Notice grace as well as knowledge.** Grace, as used here, **has reference to ability.** The child of God is commanded to grow in his

performance as well as in knowledge. A little child naturally grows in his ability as he becomes older. **(+)** Once he had to be hand-fed but now he is able to feed himself. Once he was fearful and uncertain but now he has confidence and assurance. **It came through the natural process of growth.**
3. **The grace of giving.** The church at Corinth had a rough beginning, but through the ministry of Paul it grew into one of the greatest churches in the world. In II Corinthians 8:7, Paul is commending them for their spiritual growth and improvements. He told them that **they had grown in "everything;"** in faith, in utterance, in knowledge, in their love toward him and please take note, **"ye abound in this grace also"** referring to their growth in giving. **(+)** The verse is teaching the natural process of the growth of a child of God which includes the ability to grow in the ability to give. This means that the child of God can and should grow in the ability to give today.

B. COMETH BY KNOWLEDGE (Hearing)
1. **Knowledge of God's procedure.** "Faith cometh by hearing and hearing by the Word of God." (Romans 10:17.) God's procedure of growth in a child of God comes through hearing the Word of God. When a child of God learns the Word of God, it produces a growth within the child of God.
2. **Knowledge of God's promises.** It is marvelous at the transformation which takes place within the being of a new convert as he learns of God's love and promises.
3. **Knowledge of God's provisions.** The promises speaks of God provision for the well-being of his child. When the new convert begins to realize who

he is (God's child), what he has (all of God's power and provision), and what he will possess forever, it produces tremendous change and growth in his life.

C. **CONSUMMATED THROUGH EXERCISE.**

All the **promises** and provisions which God offers to the child of God are **meaningless** unless they are accepted. One must believe and exercise faith in order to claim the promises. "Without faith it is impossible to please Him [God]." (Heb. 11:6)

1. **God said, "prove me."** In Malachi 3:10, God challenges his people to prove Him! The subject under consideration is "tithes and offerings" and God is boldly promising to bless them if they will only exercise their faith and obey. This is only one of many such promises which God makes to the believers! These promises are *given* to stimulate one to exercise his faith and accept or do God's will. "Faith without works is dead." (James 2:17) The emphasis in the Bible is to be a **doer** of the Word, not a hearer only. (James 1:22) **(+)**
2. **God's proven plan.** There may be other good plans to get God's people to give liberally to God and missions but the one that the writer prefers is called, "Faith Promise." This plan is taken directly from the Bible and if implemented and followed properly will cause the members of the local church to both grow in faith and in giving.

   A church sets aside a time in which missionaries come to the church for special services. During that time they stress the promises of God toward those who, by faith, will obey Him. Through the combination of the missionaries helping the people see the needs of their fields, the promises of God's blessing upon those who give; a challenge is made.

The challenge is - by faith. Set a certain amount such as $1, $5, $50 per week and as God supplies that amount; give it into the special mission account. This amount is above the tithe and offering which they are already giving. As God supplies that amount, they give it.

Many churches, as well as individuals, have been transformed by this "Faith Promise" principle. **(+)** One grows through knowledge (learning about the need and as well as God's promised provision) and then by faith (exercise) doing it.

III. FINANCIAL OBLIGATION VIEWED AS AN ETERNAL INVESTMENT

THURSDAY
A. MANY GIVE OUT OF HABIT.

1. **It is Sunday** - give. Many have gone to church so long that it is a routine or habit. May I quickly add, it is a good habit, but still a habit.
2. **It is offering time - give.** Each Sunday the ushers come forward, the musician plays and it is time to give; so they give.
3. **It is need time - give.** It is not unusual in the average church to have some special need arise. The offering plate is passed and people respond by giving. It is the thing to do. So we do it!

B. MANY GIVE BECAUSE IT IS COMMANDED (+)

1. **Command of what?** "Bring all the tithes into the storehouse". (Mal. 3:10) God commands it and we obey by doing it.
2. **Command of when?** "Upon the first day of the week let every one of you lay by him in store, as God has prospered him." (I Corinthians 16:2) It is the

first day of the week, Sunday, so we obey God's command and give!
3. **Command of why?** "To prove the sincerity of your love". (II Corinthians 8:8) The child of God expresses his love to his heavenly father by his obedience in giving.
4. **Command of where?** The tithe was brought to the storehouse (Mal 3:10) in the Old Testament era and to the local church in the New Testament. Judas was the first Treasurer.

Thank God for the many who give because the Word of God commands it. They know what, when, why and where to give and they do it. Praise God for these faithful, loving people but the Bible teaches a better way.

C. **MANY GIVE AS AN ETERNAL INVESTMENT.** Many Christians think hard and long about their secular investments. They will seek advice and even pay for special information or counsel But these same people give very little thought concerning the gifts of their tithes and offerings.

1. **Investment into heaven's bank.** God does have a bank and he commands His people to "Lay up for yourselves treasurers in heaven." (Matt. 6:20)

2. **Investments into the lives of others.** The book of Philippians was written by a missionary (Paul) to his sponsoring church which was located in Philippi. There are many tremendous truths presented in this missionary letter. Perhaps, the greatest truth and the one which pertains to our subject is found in Phil. 4:17. Paul speaks about the many offerings which the church gave him. He clarified why he was so grateful for their support and offerings. He said, "Not because I desire a gift [money]; but I desire

fruit [results] that may abound to your account." Paul is telling them that the support they sent time and again was more than a gift; **it was an investment in his ministry.** Their gift was a gift but it was much more than a gift. **It was an investment.** In a **manner** of speaking they had bought **shares in his missionary activities and souls won in the city of Phillipi.** They would share in the results of that great church's ministry. They would share in the results of all the ministries of those who were saved in Phillipi and later started preaching!

"Fruit that may abound to your account". Note two words: Abound and account. (+) Abound speaks of multi-level multiplication while account refers to credit or reward. The people of Phillipi who supported the missionary, Paul, will never realize the vastness and richness of their **investment** until they all stand together at the bank of heaven where the value of their account (shares) will be published.

3. **Investment depends on one's sowing (giving).** The Bible teaches that one will reap what he sows. If one sows bountifully then he will reap a large or bountiful harvest. **(+)**

    In many companies they have a payroll deductible pension plan. Each employee determines if he wants to participate in the plan and the amount he wishes to have withheld from his check. Many have tremendous retirement plans and enjoy great freedom and luxury because they invested a small amount each week which grew into a great fund through the compound interest it earned.

    Why don't you lay up for yourself treasurers in heaven. Learn to consider your giving as an

investment. Some could begin to invest $20 a week. Others may be able to invest $50 per week. Drive that old car for another year and invest (the difference between a higher car payment and your present payment) in the <u>ministry</u> of your church and missionaries. You would live just as well now, but oh the <u>difference</u> you would enjoy during the 1000 year reign of Christ. **(+)** What fruit would abound to your account --- compound interest and you would enjoy that investment **forever.**

4. **Investment which pays compound interest.** Today, the best retirement plan will cease to be the investor's **and go to another upon the investor's death.** Someone's sacrifice and careful planning is voided by death. The person will receive no personal benefit from all his planning and effort, but **God has a plan which far exceeds the best retirement plans** which was ever developed by man.

CONSIDER GOD'S SUPER-DUPER PLAN

In the last book of the Bible a representative of the bank of heaven begins to make an announcement of God's **Super Duper Investment Plan.** In the midst of his announcement concerning the plan of all plans for investors, the excited author of the plan burst through the announcement by shouting a gigantic, "YESSSS!" All of heaven stares in amazement as the Holy Spirit finishes the unbelievable announcement of benefits. "That they [investors who died] may rest from their labours; and their WORKS DO FOLLOW them." (Rev. 14:13) **(+)**

God's dear children, who had followed him by faith and invested their lives and monies in the work of

God, died! Their lives ended! Their personal giving, praying, witnessing and working ended. They died! Their physical walk among men on this earth ceased.

They followed in the steps of Stephen who cried out, "Lord Jesus, receive my Spirit," (Acts 7:59) and then went to heaven.

In Rev. 14:13, the angel declares that some of the saved died. He states their race on the earth was over. Their physical service to Christ was through. There will be no more tears, no more prayers, no more heartaches, no more persecution! They are at peace. They are resting.

It was at this point that the Holy Spirit shouted out, "YES." But look at those benefits. Look at those investments which they made in the lives and **ministries** of others. Look at that compound interest - It is doubling.... Quadrupling.... Multiplying.... **Multiplying**... MULTIPLYING. Their investments paid dividends while they were **alive,** but it is paying greater dividends after they died. **"Their works do follow them."**

SUMMARY:

It is good to be obedient and give. **(+)** God will bless you for it. **But when you learn to consider your giving as investments, it is at this point when the real joy and excitement begins.**

Notice some of the improvements in service this new knowledge will bring:

1) One will take better care of God's facilities--Why? Because it is **part of his investment.**
2) One **will pray** more earnestly for the missionary.

Why? Because the missionary **is a co-worker** who is **steward over one of your investments**. **(+)**
3) One will assist and help people more and become a greater servant. Why? Their **personal investment** is at stake; they are investing in something or service in that person's life. This understanding causes one to become responsible.
4) It is God's way for me **to lay up treasure** in heaven by helping others. **(+)**
5) It is God's way for me to **glorify Christ** by bearing more fruit. "Herein is my Father glorified that you bear much fruit." (John 15:8) **(+)**

CONCLUSION
LEARN THIS LESSON EARLY IN LIFE

As we journey through life

From the cradle to the grave

The part of your life you give

Is the ONLY PART that you save. (+)

Introduction
Monday

1. _____ shall call upon the name of the Lord shall be_____
2. He penned the_____ which reveal our _____ financial obligation within the Great Commission.
3. How shall they_____ except they be_____?
4. God spotlights the fearful responsibility of _____ member of the local church.
5. The part of life one_____ is the part that is_____.

As a Responsibility
Tuesday

1. The commission wasn't given just to_____.
2. The missionary and his _____give all.
3. Many give a waitress a bigger _____than they give to_____.

4. The_____ teaches an _____responsibility under the Great Commission.
5. The focus of the church should be on our_____. The Church's _____ is Missions.

As an Exercise of Faith
Wednesday

1. But grow in _____ and in the knowledge of our _____ Jesus Christ.
2. A_____ child naturally grows in his_____ as he becomes older.
3. "Ye abound in this_____ also" referring to their growth in_____
4. The emphasis in the _____ is to be a _____ of the Word.
5. Many_____, as well as individuals, have been transformed by this _____ principle.

As an Investment
Thursday

1. Many _____ because it is commanded.
2. Fruit that may _____ to your account. Note two words: _____ and _____.
3. If one sows _____ then he will reap a _____ or _____ harvest.
4. You would live just as_____ now but oh the_____ you would enjoy during the _____ year reign.
5. That they [investor's who have_____] may rest from their _____; and their works do _____ them"

Summary

Friday

1. It is good to be _____ and_____.
2. Because the _____ is a _____ who is_____ over one of your investments.
3. It is God's way for me to _____ up treasures in _____ by helping others.
4. Herein is my _____ glorified that _____ bear much _____
5. The part of your life you_____ is the only part that you_____

DAILY DECLARATION

I will strive to lay up treasures by investing in other ministries while I am on earth.

MEMORY VERSE

Lay not up for yourselves treasures upon earth, where moth and rust doth corrupt, and where thieves break through and steal: But lay up for yourselves treasures in heaven, where neither moth nor rust doth corrupt, and where thieves do not break through nor steal: (Matthew 6:19-20)

CHECK BLOCK AFTER REPEATING

	Mon	Tues	Wed	Thurs	Fri	Sat	Sun
A.M.							
P.M.							

MY COMMITMENT

Having studied that giving is an investment which pays eternal dividends while getting people saved from hell I make a commitment to do my best.

NAME:_____ GRADE_____

NEW BOOKS FROM NEW TESTAMENT MINISTRIES

Steph, the son of Stephans

Who am I??? What is life all about... What will bring me real fulfillment... How should I live??

WHAT IS A TRUE CHRISTIAN?

    Let us travel back to the first generation of Christians in order to find young people who found the answers to these questions. Join Steph and beautiful Priscilla as they overcome all trials and tribulation to find true happiness. In doing so you may find more than the answer to your questions.

YOU MAY FIND YOUR OWN DESTINY!

Other books by the Author

Lasting Moments of Joy are experiences which happened in a small segment of time but will produce eternal joy. The following stories happened...in moment of time

Stories for dog lovers
Stories for travelers
One story entitled "Is my baby in Hell?"
Another story about conversion of a Muslim
Stories of the helpless, hopeless who found peace

the

Stories which both the religious and non-religious will enjoy

---

"I have seen the beautiful golden sunsets and thrilled at the majestic mountains. I have been blessed with wonderful vacations with my family and been honored by my fellow man - But nothing can compare with the present-tense joy of winning a soul which will continue throughout the ages to come"

More Lasting Moments of Joy

"I have been traveling down the Gospel trail for almost 60 years and God has been so good and faithful to me. This book contains a few special moments which God used to **brighten my life**. I want to share them with you in the hope they will be a source of blessing, direction and encouragement. Much of my life will be forgotten in the shadows of the past but **these moments will live on throughout the ages to come.**"

More Lasting Moments of Joy features people saved at...

UNUSUAL PLACES: in a bathtub, phone booth, car wreck, hospital, airport, prison, over the radio, by telephone, and in the home.

UNUSUAL PEOPLE: 103 year old belly dancer; twins, a boys two fathers, 90 year old lady,

UNUSUAL EXPERIENCES: Plenty of unusual places where most would never thing a soul could be saved,

NEW CONVERT CARE DISCIPLESHIP PROGRAM

These booklets and books are presented to help the layman in the local church. We are dedicated to aiding the Pastor in strengthening members.

Other books by the Author

Through the New Convert Care Discipleship-Program, we help new converts become happy, active parts of the church family.

Through the Layman Library Series, we present books designed to train and strengthen, **Please contact author for prices.**

Books By the Author

These booklets and books are presented to help the laymen in the local church. We are dedicated to aiding the Pastor in strengthening members through the New Convert Care Discipleship Program, we help new converts become happy, active parts of the church family.

Through the Layman Library Series, we present books designed to train and strengthen. Please contact the author for prices.

* Denote Discipleship materials

THE LAYMAN LIBRARY SERIES
$1.75 each

- 100 * A Letter to a New Convert
- 102 How to Have Something in Heaven When You Get There
- 105 Incentives in Soul-winning
- 106 How to Pray So God Will Answer You
- 111 Points and Poems by Pearl – Pearl Cheeves
- 112 Foreknowledge in The Light of Soul-winning
- 113 Elected "To Go"
- 114 Predestination Promotes Soul-winning
- 115 The Ministry of Paul in the Light of Soul-winning
- 116 The Church, a Place of Protection, Love & Development

OTHER BOOKS BY DR. WILKINS

Foreknowledge, Election, & Predestination in the Light Of Soul-winning(160p)
Essentials to Successful Soul-Winning (258p)
Designed to Win (Soul winning Manuel) (120p)
Harvest Time(110p)
*Milk of The Word – (Book One) (also in Spanish) (146p)
*From Salvation to Service (also in Spanish) (40p)
*How to Be a Better Big Brother (40p)
*Big Brother Bits (40p)
*Questions Concerning Baptism (40p)
*Four Tremendous Truths (61p)
*The Mission of The Church - Book Two (198p)
Healing Words for Lonely People
How To Raise A King (64p)
*Healing Words for Hurting people (120p)
Thy Kingdom Come (46p)
The Truth About Hell (101p)
The Kindergarten Phase of Eternity (170p)
The Final Flight (50p)
The Short Race Home (50p)
Not Even a Nickel, Just A Penny (Testimony of Penny Wilkins)(40p)
A Struggle to Peace (Cindy Benson) (58p)
*The Meat of The Word - Book Three (186p)
God's Cure for Our Nation (218p)
God's Brilliant Plan to Reach Fallen Man
The Scriptural Goal of Teaching God's Word (91p)
To Circle The Earth Once Again (157p)

For a Complete list and price information contact us:

Dr. James Wilkins, Director

New Testament Ministries

Dr. James Wilkins
PO Box 1999
Santa Cruz, NM 87567
(505) 747-6917
leatherman_wave@yahoo.com

www.JamesWilkins.org